Creating Beaded
& Wire Earrings

Creating Beaded & Wire Earrings

35 step-by-step projects
for dazzling, stylish earrings

Linda Jones

CICO BOOKS
LONDON NEW YORK

To the two most precious things in my life, my sons, Ben and Charlie, who keep me focused and level headed (most of the time!) and provide me with the motivation and desire to keep learning and be creative.

Published in 2011 by CICO Books
An imprint of Ryland Peters & Small
519 Broadway, 5th Floor, New York, NY 10012
20–21 Jockey's Fields, London WC1R 4BW

www.cicobooks.com

10 9 8 7 6 5 4 3 2 1

Text © Linda Jones 2011
Design and photography © CICO Books 2011

A CIP catalog record for this book is available from the Library of Congress and the British Library.

ISBN: 978-1-907563-23-2

Printed in China

Design: David Fordham
Photography: Geoff Dann, Stuart West, Jacqui Hurst, Gloria Nicol, Caroline Arber, and David Munns
Styling: Luis Peral-Aranda, Denise Brock, Deborah Schneebeli-Morrell, Julie Hailey, Sammie Bell
Illustration: Stephen Dew

Contents

Introduction

If I were to go out without wearing earrings, I would feel naked!
It's the one item of jewelry that I love to wear and that drew me
to creating wire jewelry in the first place. Don't let anyone tell
you that you have too many earrings—when you've mastered how
to create your own, there is no limit!

Ready-made head pins, ear wires, and jump rings are all readily
available from suppliers, making the task extremely simple.
However, if you want to stamp your individuality on what you
wear, learn a few extra techniques, which can be found within this
book, and create the entire earring from scratch, with just a spool
of wire and a sprinkling of beads. Ear wires and head pins can
become a major part of the design and integral to the overall style.

Once you've mastered a few basic wire-working rules and become
proficient with your pliers, the variations and combinations are
endless. Round-, flat-, and chain-nose pliers, together with a good
pair of wire cutters and a hammer and steel block, are your essential

These beautiful earrings in the
style of Egyptian hieroglyphics
can be found on page 88.

tool kit. If you're making your own ear wires, a pin vice, fitted with a cup burr, is also useful for sanding off the ends of the ear wires, with a little sanding paper to complete to a perfectly smooth finish.

Earrings don't take long to make—you can create a pair in 15 minutes from your kitchen table or in your lunch hour at work—and they also make perfect, personalized gifts for friends and family, so there's no excuse not to be able to fit this in to your busy life! I do hope the variety and range of projects within the six chapters will provide inspiration not only for earring designs, but for necklaces and bracelets, too. I know I will never stop learning and creating new configurations. Plus, the Earrings Gallery on pages 124–5 will give you a further taste of how you can experiment with other structures and styles.

Above are just a few examples of the wealth of inspiration to be found in the Earrings gallery on pages 124–5. Below are the gorgeous projects for Birthstone Earrings (page 110) and Tassel Earrings (page 103).

Tools

One of the joys of making wire and beaded jewelry is that you require very little in the way of specialty tools and equipment—and everything you need is readily available from craft suppliers, mail-order catalogs, and, of course, the Internet at very affordable prices. Here are my suggestions for a basic tool kit.

Hammer and flat steel stake

These tools are used to flatten and toughen wire motifs (see page 13). Specialty jewelry hammers are generally smaller and lighter than general-purpose household hammers, but you can use any hammer as long as one end has a flat, smooth, polished surface. Steel stakes can be bought from specialty jewelry stores, but any flat steel surface will do provided the top surface has no bumps or abrasions —otherwise the wire will pick up any irregularities that are present.

Pliers

From top to bottom: Round-, flat-, and chain-nose pliers. Round-nose pliers have round, tapered shafts; they are used to coil and bend wire into small loops and curves and to make jump rings. Chain-nose and flat-nose pliers are both used to grip the wire firmly as you work and to bend it at right angles and angular shapes. However, chain-nose pliers are tapered and narrow and therefore are extremely useful when working on intricate, more delicate pieces. They are also essential for neatening ends.

Ring mandrel or triblet

Available from specialty jewelry stores, a mandrel is used to form circular shapes such as rings and bangles. Alternatively, shape your wire around any cylindrical object of the appropriate size.

Wire cutters

Several kinds of wire cutter are available, but I find that "side cutters" are the most useful as they have small, tapered blades that can cut into small spaces. Remember to hold the cutters perpendicular to the wire when cutting to achieve a clean, flush cut.

Jig and pegs

A jig consists of a base board with evenly spaced holes and moveable pegs with tops of different diameters, which you arrange in a pattern. You then wrap wire around the pegs to create a wire design. Some jig grids are based on a square and some on the diagonal, so you may have to alter the project patterns slightly to suit your make of jig.

Materials

There is such a wonderful array of beautiful beads, colorful wires, and findings available that you will be spoilt for choice! If this is your first step into wire jewelry making, you'll enjoy bead browsing. In fact, the difficulty will be deciding when to stop!

Wire

Wire is available in many thicknesses, types, and colors. Colored, copper, and plated wires can be bought from most craft and hobby stores, as well as from bead suppliers. With the exception of precious metal, wire is generally sold in spools of a pre-measured length. Precious-metal wire is bought by length, the price being calculated by weight.

Colored wires are usually copper based, with enamel coatings, which means that they cannot be hammered or over-manipulated as this might remove the surface color and look unsightly. Instead of precious-metal wires, I almost always use gold- or silver-plated wires, which are far less expensive. The only exception to this is if you need to file the wire, as filing the end will expose the copper core underneath the plating and look unattractive. Therefore, sterling-silver wire is essential for this type of design.

All these kinds of wire come in different thicknesses. Depending on where you buy your wire, different measurements are used to denote the thickness of the wire. The chart below will enable you to convert quickly from one system to another. The most commonly used general-purpose wire for jewelry making is 20-gauge (0.8 mm).

28-gauge (0.4mm)   Binding, knitting, and weaving
24-gauge (0.6mm)   Threading small delicate beads; binding and twisting
20-gauge (0.8mm)   General-purpose jewelry work
18-gauge (1.0mm)   Chunkier pieces and ring shanks
16-gauge (1.2mm)   Bolder, chunkier jewelry
14-gauge (1.5mm)   Very chunky, metallic wire jewelry

Findings

Findings is the term used to describe ready-made components such as ear wires and clips (see left), as well as chains, barrettes, and so on. They can be bought from craft and hobby stores. Alternatively, you can make your own handmade ear wires (see right for design ideas, and page 15 for how to make your own spiral fish-hook ear wires).

Beads

Beads are made from all kinds of materials including glass, porcelain, plastic, metal, wood, and bone. Specialist bead stores contain thousands of different sizes and types, arranged by both color and size, and I defy anyone to visit such a store without buying something! Semiprecious chip stones and bone- or wood-effect beads are lovely beads to use. Tiny seed beads—usually sold in tubes—are useful as "stopper" beads but, because they are so tiny, if you want them to have any impact in a design you generally need to string several together. Pre-drilled shells also make lovely beads—and you can even use objects without a pre-drilled hole, such as small pebbles, by wrapping wire around them.

When buying beads, always check that the wire you intend to use fits through the bead hole, as there is no correlation between the size of a bead and the diameter of its hole. If you can't find beads that exactly match the ones that I've used in the projects in this book, buy something of a similar size.

Basic Techniques

Using a jig

Before you try a jig project, place your pegs in your chosen design and then wrap a piece of cord or string approximately the same gauge as the wire that will be used around the pegs, following the pattern. Measure the amount of cord or string that you have used so that you know how much wire you will need to make the project, and then cut your wire to this length. To work harden your jig unit, flatten it in your flat-nose pliers or gently "stroke" hammer (see page 13) the outer extremities of the motif.

1 Following your chosen pattern, place the pegs in the jig. Using your round-nose pliers, form a link at one end of your length of wire and slip it over the first peg, securing it in place.

2 Pull the wire around the pegs, following the pattern, pushing it down in order to keep the shape reasonably flat. Carefully remove the wire unit from the pegs, and gently "stroke" hammer the outer areas to work harden (see page 13).

Making bead links

The basic principle is to construct a neat loop of wire (known as a "link") at each end of the bead, which is then used to suspend the bead from an ear wire or to connect one bead to another.

When you've threaded the bead, hold each link firmly in the jaws of your pliers and twist until both links face the same way—otherwise they will twist around when linked together as a chain.

1 Working from the spool, thread your chosen bead onto the wire, leaving about ½ in. (1 cm) of wire extending on each side.

2 Remove the bead and cut the wire with your wire cutters.

Neatening ends

When you've wrapped one piece of wire around another, it's important to neaten the ends to prevent any sharp pieces from sticking out and snagging on clothing or scratching the wearer.

3 Thread the bead back onto the cut wire. Holding the wire vertically, with the bead in the center, use the tips of your round-nose pliers to bend the wire at a right angle, at the point where it touches the bead.

4 Hold the end of the bent wire tightly with your round-nose pliers and curl it round to form a small circle, following the contour of your pliers. Do this in several short movements; reposition the pliers as needed. Repeat Steps 3–4 to form another link at the other end of the bead.

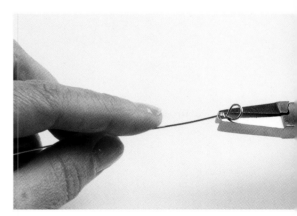

1 Snip the wire as close as possible to the stem, and then press it firmly with your flat- or chain-nose pliers to flatten it against the piece of jewelry. For an extra-smooth finish, use a small needle file to file away any roughness.

Making a head pin

If you want to suspend a bead from a chain, you only need a suspension link at one end of the bead. At the other end, you need to make what is known as a "head pin," which is virtually invisible but prevents the bead from slipping off the wire.

The head pin (shown here on the right-hand end of the bead) is unobtrusive, but it prevents the bead from slipping off the wire.

1 Working from the spool, thread your chosen bead onto the wire and let it slip down, leaving the end exposed.

2 Using the tips of your round-nose pliers, make a tiny curl at one end of the wire. Squeeze this curl flat with your flat-nose pliers to create a knob of doubled wire.

3 Push your bead right up to the head pin and snip the wire, leaving a stem ½ in. (1 cm) long. Form a link at this end of the wire, using your round-nose pliers. If the hole in the bead slips over the head pin, bend the head pin at a right angle, so that the bead sits on top of it like a tiny shelf. (Alternatively, slide on a small seed bead to act as a stopper.)

Above are some examples of handmade head pins. Top row, from left to right: standard, closed spiral, flattened spiral; bottom row, from left to right: hammered end, "Greek key," triangle.

Work hardening

Work hardening means toughening the wire so that it can take the strain of being worn without distorting and falling apart. One method is to hammer the piece on a clean, smooth, dent-free steel stake. Use a nylon hammer or place a cloth over the piece before you hammer when work hardening colored wire, as the colored coating can rub off. This technique is not suitable for small jump rings or links, as it will distort their shape.

1 Place your piece on the stake and "stroke" hammer it, bringing the flat part of the hammer down at 90° to the piece. Hammer your piece standing up, so that the hammer head hits the wire squarely, rather than at an angle, which could create texturing in the metal. After several strokes you will see the wire flattening, spreading, and work hardening.

Making spirals

There are two kinds of spiral: open and closed. Each is formed in the same way, the only difference being whether or not any space is left between the coils. Both types of spiral begin by curling a circle at the end of the wire. If you want to make a closed spiral without a center hole, make a head pin first and curl the remaining wire around the doubled-up end.

A closed spiral has no gaps between the coils. An open spiral is made in the same way, but evenly spaced gaps are left between the coils.

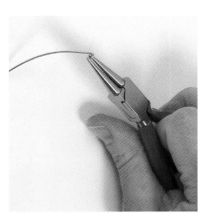

1 Begin by curling a small circle at the end of the wire, using the tips of your round-nose pliers. Make this circle as round as possible, as the rest of the spiral will be shaped around it.

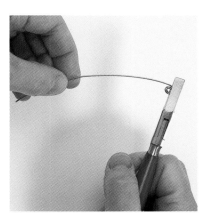

2 Grip the circle tightly in the jaws of your flat-nose pliers and begin curling the wire around it. For a closed spiral, shown here, butt each coil up against the previous one. For an open spiral, leave an even space between each coil.

3 When the spiral is the size you want, leave about ½ in. (1 cm) of wire to form a suspension link, curling the projecting end of wire into a small loop in the opposite direction to the spiral.

Making jump rings

Jump rings are used to connect units together. You can buy them ready made, but it is well worth learning how to make them yourself as you can then match the jump rings to the color and size of wire that you are using. It is also much less expensive to make them yourself!

Jump rings are made by forming a wire coil around the shaft of your round-nose pliers, out of which you snip individual rings as required. When you bring the wire around the pliers to begin forming the second ring of the coil, it needs to go below the first coil, nearer your hand. This keeps the wire on the same part of the pliers every time. If you bring the wire around and above the first ring of the coil, the jump rings will taper, following the shape of the pliers' shaft.

You can also make jump rings by wrapping wire around a cylindrical object such as a knitting needle, large nail, or the barrel of a pen, depending on the diameter required.

1 Working from the spool, wrap wire five or six times around one shaft of your round-nose pliers, curling it around the same part of the pliers every time to create an even coil.

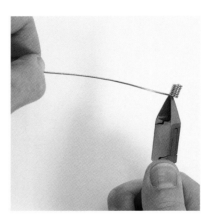

2 Remove the coil from the pliers and then cut it off from the spool of wire using your wire cutters.

3 Find the cut end and, using your wire cutters, snip upward into the next ring of the coil above, thereby cutting off a full circle. Continue cutting each ring off the coil in turn to obtain more jump rings.

Using jump rings to connect units

1 Using your flat-nose pliers, open one of the jump rings sidewise (like a door), so that you do not distort the shape. Loop the open jump ring through the links of the beads and close it with flat-nose pliers. The two ends of the jump rings should move just past one another, as the wire will spring back slightly when you remove the pliers. If you don't push the wires hard enough you will end up with a gap, which may mean that the beads will work loose.

Creating a spiral fish-hook ear wire

The amount of wire required for each hook is totally dependent on the weight and size of the bead you are going to suspend—large beaded earrings will require a longer hook than small, light ones.

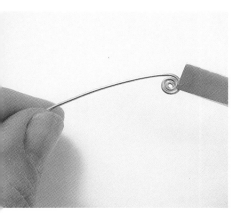

1 Cut approximately 4 in. (10 cm) of 20-gauge (0.8mm) wire for each hook. Create a tiny head pin at the end (see page 12) and continue curling the wire around itself to form a closed spiral (see page 13).

2 Using the tips of your round-nose pliers, bend a kink in the wire, just by the spiral, so that it sits central on the stem.

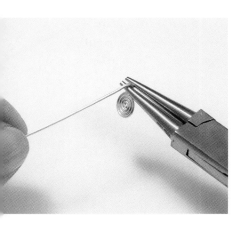

3 Place your round-nose pliers just by the spiral stem and bend into a loop, so that the stem wire is nearly touching the spiral.

4 Using a pencil or similar cylindrical mandrel, bend the stem wire around to form the earring hook.

Tips for making spiral fish-hook ear wires:

- To get rid of any scratchy ends, use a needle file and wet-and-dry paper. Alternatively, if you have a cup burr fitted onto a pin vice, this is also ideal, followed by some filing.
- If the hook parts of the wires are too soft, you can hammer them on a steel stake to work harden them (see page 13).
- To shape the ends into a curve, place the widest part of your round-nose pliers at the end of each hook.
- If you're suspending a heavy or long decoration from the hooks, add a rubber "butterfly" back to ensure that the hooks cannot fall out of the ears.

There is a whole range of other types of ear wires you can make yourself—ear wires are relatively simple to create by hand. Below are some examples to inspire you to make your own.

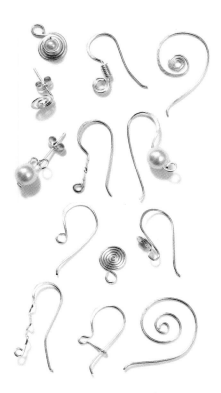

Chapter 1

Fashion Focus

Express your individual style and personality by wearing statement earrings to complement all your outfits. All the projects in this chapter can be created with your own choice of beads to blend with your favorite color combinations.

Teardrop Earrings

The tapered shape of this design, with its delicate internal spirals, is very elegant and can be suspended either way up. The "teardrop" unit also looks dramatic as a necklace centerpiece, suspended either from a cord (for a casual look) or from a chain.

You will need

20-gauge (0.8mm) and 28-gauge (0.4mm) silver wire

2 x 10mm gray feature beads

2 x 15mm blue/gray drop pendant beads

2 x 5mm blue/gray round beads

2 x ready-made ear wires

Wire cutters

Round- and flat-nose pliers

Mandrel or dowel about 1 in. (2.5 cm) in diameter

Hammer and steel stake (optional)

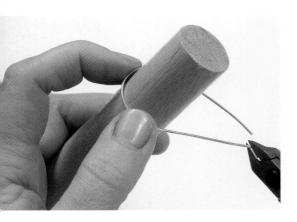

1 For each earring, wrap the end of a spool of 20-gauge (0.8mm) silver wire around a mandrel or dowel about 1 in. (2.5 cm) in diameter to form a loop, bringing the ends together to a point. Cut the wire to make the teardrop-shaped frame.

2 Wrap one end of the wire around the other, cut off any excess, and neaten the end (see page 11), leaving the second wire projecting. If you wish, gently "stroke" hammer (see page 13) the outer frame to work harden it.

3 Curl the projecting wire into a link (see page 11). This will be the bottom of the earring.

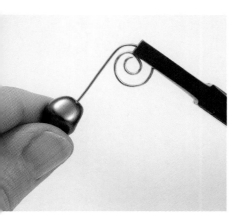

4 Cut two 5–6-in. (12.5–15-cm) lengths of 20-gauge (0.8mm) wire. Thread a 10mm gray feature bead onto each one and form an open spiral (see page 13) on each side, curling the wire in opposite directions like a figure eight. If you wish, "stroke" hammer (see page 13) the spirals, taking care not to hit the central bead.

5 For each earring, cut two 2-in. (5-cm) lengths of 28-gauge (0.4mm) wire. Use each one to bind the spirals to the top and bottom of the teardrop frame. Cut off any excess and neaten the ends (see page 11).

6 Thread the 15mm blue/gray pendant bead onto 20-gauge (0.8mm) wire and form a head pin at one end and a link at the other (see pages 11 and 12). Open the link on the pendant bead, hook it through the link at the base of the teardrop frame, then close the link with your flat-nose pliers.

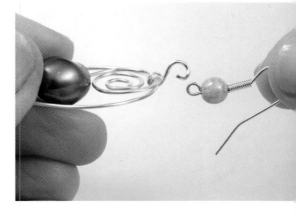

7 Cut a small piece of 20-gauge (0.8mm) wire. Using round-nose pliers, curl each end into a link (see page 11), curling the wire in opposite directions to form a figure eight.

8 Open one link of the figure eight, hook it under the binding wire at the top of the teardrop frame, then close it again.

9 Undo the link at the end of the ready-made ear wires, straighten out the wire, and remove any beads. Slide a 5mm blue/gray round bead onto each ear wire, then re-make the link. Open the other link on the figure eight made in Step 7, hook it into the bottom link of the ear wire, then close it again.

Make a matching pendant necklace by connecting together different-shaped beads in the same grays and silvers via jump rings, and suspending a larger version of the teardrop motif from the center.

Bead-Pod Earrings

This design, which was inspired by flower seeds encased in a papery pod, is ideal for setting off any bicone-shaped beads or crystals that you have in your stash. Framing beads with wire in this way is an effective way of making them more prominent. For something a little more lighthearted, why not use red, orange, and green beads in succession and turn them into "traffic-light" earrings?

You will need

20-gauge (0.8mm) copper and
   28-gauge (0.4mm) gold-plated
   wire
6 x 6mm bicone crystal beads
2 x 10mm crystal hearts
2 x ready-made flat-backed
   earring posts and butterfly
   backs
Wire cutters
Round-, chain-, and flat-nose pliers
Superglue

1 For each earring, cut a 5-in. (12.5-cm) length of 20-gauge (0.8mm) copper wire. Placing your round-nose pliers in the center, bend the wire in half. Using the tips of your chain-nose pliers, pinch the wires together just under the round-nose pliers to form a loop, with the projecting wires running parallel to each other.

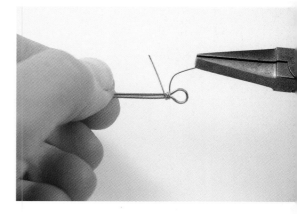

2 Cut a 1½-in. (4-cm) length of 28-gauge (0.4mm) gold-plated wire and bind it around the doubled wires, just under the loop. Cut off any excess and neaten the end (see page 11).

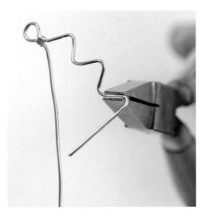

3 Place your flat-nose pliers by the binding and bend the wire into an angular shape. Continue bending the wire into a zig-zag pattern until you have three complete zig-zags on one side. You should have about ½ in. (1 cm) of wire left unbent.

4 Repeat Step 3 on the other wire to create a mirror image of the zig-zags. Straighten one wire stem, then wrap the other wire around that stem to secure. Cut off any excess wire from the wrap, and neaten the end (see page 11).

5 Using your round-nose pliers, form a link (see page 11) at the end of the straight wire.

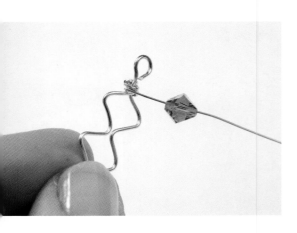

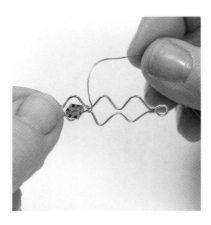

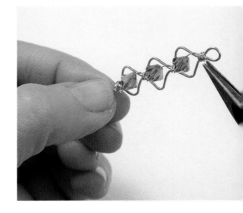

6 Cut 5 in. (12.5 cm) of 28-gauge (0.4mm) gold-plated wire. Wrap one end around the binding that you did in Step 2. Using flat-nose pliers, press the end to flatten it against the binding so that no sharp edges protrude. Thread a 6mm bicone crystal onto the wire and position it in the center of the unit, in the space between the first zig-zag.

7 Bind again where the two ends of the first zig-zag meet, to secure the bead.

8 Thread your second and third beads onto the frame in the same way, again binding the wire around the frame after each bead. Cut off any excess wire and neaten the end (see page 11).

9 Make a large jump ring from 20-gauge (0.8mm) wire (see page 14). Open the jump ring, hook on a crystal heart, and attach it to one end of the bead pod.

If you prefer, you could attach a spiral and bead at the end instead of a crystal heart.

10 Working from the spool of 20-gauge (0.8mm) copper wire, make a closed spiral (see page 13) about ¼ in. (5mm) in diameter. Cut the wire from the spool, leaving about ½–¾ in. (1.5–2 cm) projecting. Curl this projecting wire into a link (see page 11). Using your flat-nose pliers, turn the link so that it sits at 90° to the spiral.

11 Using Superglue, glue the spiral to the flat end of an earring post. Leave the glue to dry completely.

12 Open the link on the spiral, hook it through the link at the opposite end of the bead pod to the crystal heart, and then close the link again to complete the earring.

Yin-Yang Earrings

The curving wire of this design is inspired by the yin-yang symbol, which, in ancient Chinese philosophy, represents the opposing forces that maintain the harmony of the universe. In Chinese culture, jade is considered the most precious of all stones and symbolizes nobility, perfection, constancy, and immortality—so I incorporated jade-green beads and a butterfly pendant into my design to continue the Chinese theme.

You will need

20-gauge (0.8mm) silver wire
4 x 10mm round green beads
2 x 8mm butterfly-shaped beads
2 x ready-made earring posts and
   butterfly backs
Wire cutters
Round- and flat-nose pliers
Hammer and steel stake

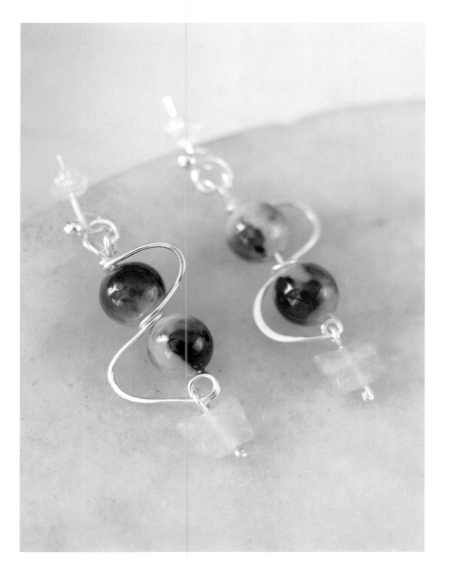

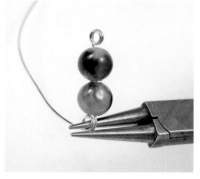

1 For each earring, thread two 10mm beads onto a spool of 20-gauge (0.8mm) silver wire. Wrap the wire twice around the same part of the shaft of your round-nose pliers to make two small coils, as when making jump rings (see page 14). Push the beads right up to the coils, then form a link (see page 11) at the end of the last threaded bead.

2 Place the widest part of your round-nose pliers by the side of the last threaded bead and form the wire into a curved shape on one side of the bead. (Alternatively, pull the wire into shape using your fingers.) Wrap the wire one and a half times around the stem, in between the two green beads.

3 Repeat Step 2 by the side of the first bead that you threaded onto the wire, this time forming the curve on the opposite side. Secure the end of the wire by wrapping it around the top of the stem. Cut the wire off the spool and neaten the end (see page 11). "Stroke" hammer (see page 13) the rounded ends of the curves, being careful not to hammer the beads.

4 Thread one of the small butterfly beads with 20-gauge (0.8mm) wire, forming a link at one end and a head pin at the other (see pages 11 and 12). Open the link, hook it over the link at the base of the earring, then close it again.

5 Using the tips of your flat-nose pliers, carefully separate the two coils at the top of the earring so that they form a V-shape. Make a large jump ring (see page 14) from 20-gauge (0.8mm) wire. Open the jump ring, thread it through the two top coils, and close it again. Connect the earring to a ready-made ear post.

Looped Bead Earrings

These earrings can be made in various sizes simply by altering the length of the wire spirals and the size of the bead in the center. As wires are available in a wide range of colors, you can match them to almost any outfit. For a really dramatic statement, you could even create two colored spirals, one suspended within the other.

You will need
24-gauge (0.6mm) black wire
20-gauge (0.8mm) silver wire
2 x 6mm black oval beads
2 x ready-made ear wires
Wire cutters
Round- and flat-nose pliers
Spiral Bead Maker or Coiling Gizmo (optional)
Mandrel or dowel about ¾ in. (2 cm) in diameter)

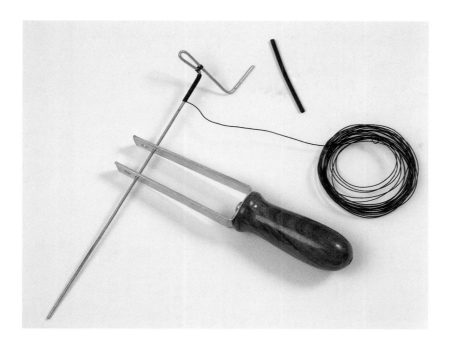

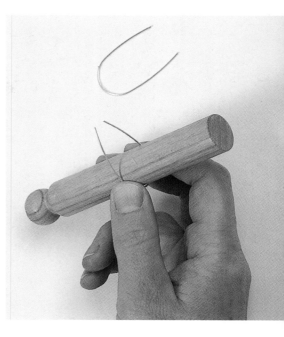

1 Using a Spiral Bead Maker or Coiling Gizmo, spiral about 2½ in. (6–7 cm) of 24-gauge (0.6mm) black wire for each earring. Alternatively, coil the black wire around a thin knitting needle.

2 Cut two 3¼-in. (8.25-cm) lengths of 20-gauge (0.8mm) silver wire and curve each one into a U-shape by bending it around a mandrel or dowel.

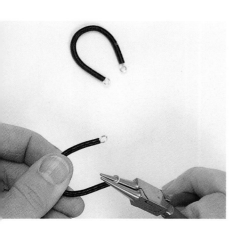

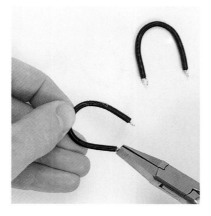

3 Feed a black spiral onto each curved silver wire. Using round-nose pliers, make a link at each end of the curved silver wires (see page 11).

4 Using flat-nose pliers, twist the links at 90° so that they face each other.

5 Mold the looped frames around the mandrel or dowel to re-shape them, making sure that the top links sit close together.

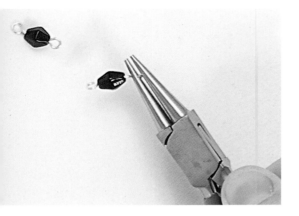

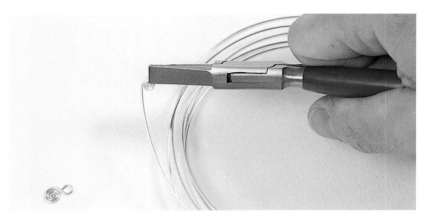

6 Thread each black bead onto a 1½-in. (4-cm) length of 20-gauge (0.8mm) silver wire and make a link at each end (see page 11).

7 Using 20-gauge (0.8mm) silver wire, make two small, closed spirals (see page 13). Make a link at one end of each spiral and connect one spiral to the base of each bead.

8 Make two large jump rings from 20-gauge (0.8mm) silver wire (see page 14), and thread them through the links at the top of each earring, suspending the bead-and-spiral unit in the center.

9 To complete the earrings, connect them to ready-made ear wires.

Sixties Hoop Earrings

There are endless variations on this classic yet modern design. You can create the hoops in wires of different colors, or alternatively, beads can be threaded onto the hoops for extra color and ornamentation.

You will need

20-gauge (0.8mm) wire (or 18-gauge/1mm wire for a chunkier look)

28-gauge (0.4mm) fine binding wire

Wire cutters

2 x ready-made ear wires

Round- and flat-nose pliers

3 cylindrical dowels of varying diameters to shape your hoops

Masking tape

1 Begin by wrapping 20-gauge (0.8mm) wire around the three cylindrical dowels to form wire hoops with different diameters.

2 When the hoops are cut, the circles will spring open. Spend a little time closing and forming the wire into even circles.

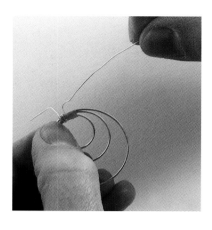

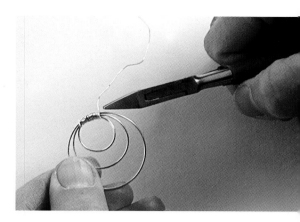

3 Position the three hoops within each other and tape together at the top with masking tape to secure and to hide the join of the circles.

4 Cut a generous length of 28-gauge (0.4mm) fine binding wire and wrap this tightly over the masking tape join to conceal it.

5 Using wire cutters, cut the end of the fine binding wire close to the hoops, ensuring that the cut end does not protrude outward.

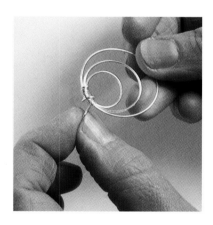

6 To create the suspension hook, cut a 1-in. (2.5-cm) length of 20-gauge (0.8mm) wire and form an "S" link.

7 Carefully open up one end of the "S" link and thread it through the middle of the three bound hoops, close to the binding.

8 Using your flat-nose pliers, squeeze the end of the "S" link around the top to secure. Finish by connecting the earrings to ready-made silver ear wires.

Pink Daisy Earrings

Pink and perky, these colorful little flower earrings are the perfect piece of spring- or summertime jewelry. Why not make several pairs, in different colors, to match different outfits? You can make these earrings with just a single daisy, or link two or more daisies and wire spirals together for a longer version.

You will need
20-gauge (0.8 mm) dark pink wire
Wire cutters
Round- and flat-nose pliers
2 x ready-made ear wires

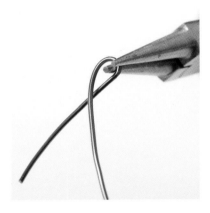

1 Working directly from the spool, form a loop around the shaft of your round-nose pliers about 1 in. (2.5 cm) from the end of the wire.

2 Cross the wire over the first loop and make a second loop, opposite the first.

3 Repeat the process, looping the wire around the pliers so that the loops sit opposite each other each time, until you have five or six "petals." Cut the wire off the spool, leaving about 1½ in. (4 cm) extending. Turn the flower shape over and wrap the short end of wire (left from making the first loop in Step 1) around the center of the flower.

4 Press the wrapped wire flat with your flat-nose pliers to secure. Cut off any excess and neaten the ends (see page 11). Using your fingers, adjust the petals until you are satisfied with the flower shape.

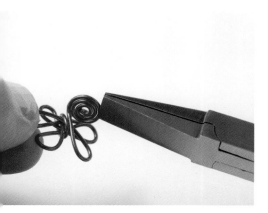

5 Using the tips of your round-nose pliers, curl a hook at the end of the extending wire. Using your flat-nose pliers, squeeze the hook onto the extending wire like a head pin, and then continue coiling the wire around itself to create a tight spiral. Press the spiral onto the center of the flower. Repeat Steps 1–5 to make the second earring.

6 Make a closed spiral from pink 20-gauge (0.8mm) wire (see page 13) and link it into one petal of the daisy. Attach a ready-made ear wire to a petal on the opposite side of the daisy.

Chapter 2

Vintage Fun

The projects in this chapter are reminiscent
of a by-gone era... take a nostalgic trip into the
past and add a touch of originality to your
jewelry collection.

Candelabra Earrings

Candelabras are synonymous with sparkling elegance and style, so I used crystal beads for these earrings. Crystal and pearl combinations would make very pretty wedding earrings; alternatively, try black crystals on gold wire for stunning eveningwear.

You will need

20-gauge (0.8mm) silver wire

2 x 10mm, 2 x 6mm, and 4 x 8mm bicone blue crystals

2 x 4mm round silver beads

2 x ready-made ear wires

Wire cutters

Round-, chain-, and flat-nose pliers

Masking tape

Hammer and steel stake

1 For each earring, cut one 2½-in. (6.5-cm) and four 2-in. (5-cm) lengths of 20-gauge (0.8mm) silver wire. Place all the wires together in a bunch and secure with a sliver of masking tape, with all the wires aligning at one end and the long wire sticking out at the other end.

2 Using round-nose pliers and working from the spool of wire, make a coil of 20-gauge (0.8mm) wire just long enough to cover the masking tape, in the same way as when making jump rings (see page 14). Slide the coil over the end of the bunch of wires to hide the masking tape.

3 Using chain-nose pliers, squeeze the first and last loops of the coil to secure it around the bunch of wires.

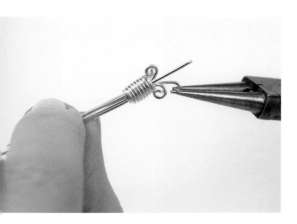

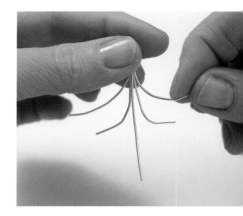

4 Above the coil, using the tips of your round-nose pliers, curl the end of each short wire into a small spiral (see page 13). Using flat-nose pliers, flatten the spirals against the coil.

5 Curl the end of the long wire into a link (see page 11).

6 Below the coil, curl each short wire outward by wrapping it around a cylindrical object such as a pencil and then adjusting the shape with your fingers. Leave the long central wire uncurled.

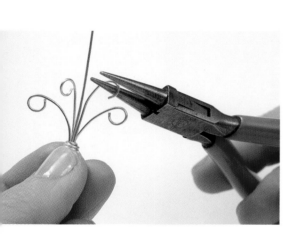

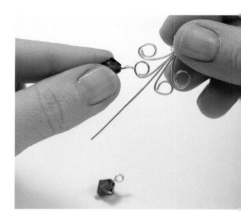

7 Using your round-nose pliers, curl the end of each short wire into a large circle.

8 Using flat-nose pliers, curl the circles around a little more so that the ends overlap—as if starting a spiral (see page 13).

9 Thread four 8mm bicone crystals (two for each earring) with wire, forming a link at one end and a head pin at the other (see pages 11 and 12). Open up the links and hook them over the bottom two circles on each earring. Close the links again with your flat-nose pliers.

10 Thread the remaining beads onto the long center wire in this order: 10mm bicone crystal, 6mm bicone crystal, 4mm silver bead. Form a head pin (see page 12) at the end of the wire to hold the beads in place.

11 To connect the units to ready-made ear wires, open the link at the bottom of the ear wire, hook it into the link at the top of the "candelabra," and close with flat-nose pliers.

For a slightly more elaborate and glitzy look, add an extra clear glass bead above the coiled stem and suspend a drop bead from a jump ring at the base of the "candelabra."

Bead Bunch Earrings

These elegant crystal and pearl earrings are inspired by sixteenth-century designs. The more beads you add, the more elaborate they will be. Make the matching necklace and wear together for sophisticated style.

You will need

20-gauge (0.8mm) gold-plated wire

Clear crystal and pearl beads, ⅛–¼ in.
   (4–5mm) in diameter

Gold-plated ready-made chain

2 x ready-made gilt ear wires

Wire cutters

Round- and flat-nose pliers

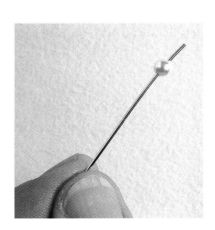

1 For each earring, cut four 2-in. (5-cm) lengths of wire. Take two crystal and two pearl beads and thread one bead onto each wire.

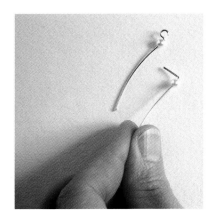

2 Bend each wire at a right angle ½ in. (1 cm) from the end, then form into a link (see page 11).

3 Create a spiral at the other end of each wire with flat-nose pliers (see page 13).

Make a matching necklace or bracelet by attaching the crystal and pearl beads to a chain. You can make it more ornate by making your own chain and adding pearls and crystals to it.

4 Link one crystal and one pearl threaded bead onto a jump ring (see page 14). Repeat this process so that you end up with two pairs of linked beads for each earring.

5 Cut a short piece of ready-made chain (about four links long) and attach one jump ring (threaded with a pair of crystal and pearl beads) to one end.

6 Thread a ready-made ear wire through the top link of the chain. Attach the jump ring with the second pair of beads to the top link of the chain, next to the ear wire. If you wish, add more beads for a fuller look.

Falling Leaves Earrings

These stylish earrings are formed from beaded leaves in autumnal shades of copper and bronze. The wire leaf can be used in other jewelry, too—when hung on a chain, it makes the perfect centerpiece for a pretty necklace. Or, why not use them as decorations for greetings cards and scrapbook layouts or as gift tags?

This variation uses tube and seed beads for a slightly more delicate look.

You will need

20- and 26-gauge (0.8mm and 0.4mm) copper wire

Approx. 28 size 11/0 gold-colored seed beads

4 x 6mm copper-colored beads

2 x ready-made ear wires

Wire cutters

Round- and flat-nose pliers

Hammer and steel stake

1 Decide how long you want the leaves to be and cut just over double that amount of 20-gauge (0.8mm) copper wire for each one. For example, to make a leaf 1½ in. (4 cm) long, you will need about 4 in. (10 cm) of wire. Bend the wire in two, just past the halfway point, so that one section is slightly longer than the other.

2 Using your flat-nose pliers, wrap the longer end of wire tightly around the shorter wire two or three times and snip off any excess, leaving the shorter wire extending by about ½ in. (1 cm).

3 At the other end of the leaf, squeeze the wires together with your flat-nose pliers, leaving a narrow channel between them.

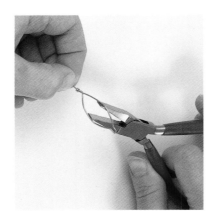

4 Place your flat-nose pliers in the space between the wires at the center of the leaf and gently pry the wires apart by opening the pliers. Using your flat-nose pliers, spend a little time adjusting the piece into a leaf shape.

5 Hammer the wire frame on your steel block to work-harden it, avoiding the wrapped end (see page 13).

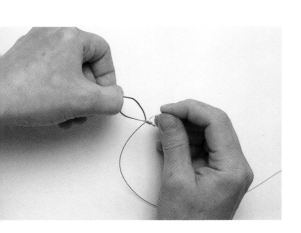

6 Curl the extending wire at the base of the leaf into a link with your round-nose pliers (see page 11). Wrap 26-gauge (0.4mm) wire around the top of the leaf (just underneath the link).

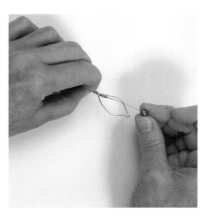

7 Pull this narrow wire straight down the center of the leaf shape and cut it off from the spool, leaving at least ½ in. (1 cm) extending beyond the end of the leaf. Thread gold seed beads onto this wire all the way up to the tip of the leaf, with one 6mm copper bead in the center as a focal bead.

8 Using your flat-nose pliers, wrap any excess wire around the end tip of the leaf a couple of times to secure it. Thread the projecting wire at the top of the leaf with a 6mm copper bead, then form a link (see page 11) to attach it to ready-made copper ear wires.

Art Deco Earrings

These Art Deco earrings have such an elegant design, with gently curving loops and hanging beads. You can easily improvise on this design by hanging it upside down or by reducing or enlarging the design.

You will need

20-gauge (0.8mm) silver-plated wire
2 x 8mm red teardrop beads
2 x ready-made ear wires
Wire cutters

Round- and flat-nose pliers
Cylindrical dowel ½ in. (12mm) in diameter)
Hammer and steel stake

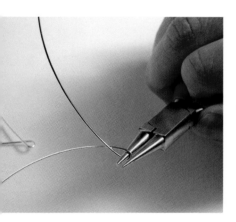

1 For each earring, cut one 5-in. (12.5-cm) length of 20-gauge (0.8mm) wire. Find the center of the wire with your round-nose pliers and cross the wires over.

2 Curl one wire loosely around the cylindrical dowel (the shaft of a thick pen will do) to create a large loop that crosses over the outer frame.

3 Form another loop on the other side of the frame in the same way; the two loops should face away from each other.

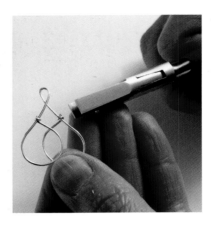

4 Using round-nose pliers, bring the projecting ends of the wire around the frame near the top central link.

5 Using flat-nose pliers, secure the wire around the main framework and neaten the ends (see page 11).

6 Gently hammer the pieces on a steel stake to straighten and flatten them. Be careful not to hammer on any crossed-over wires, since this will weaken them.

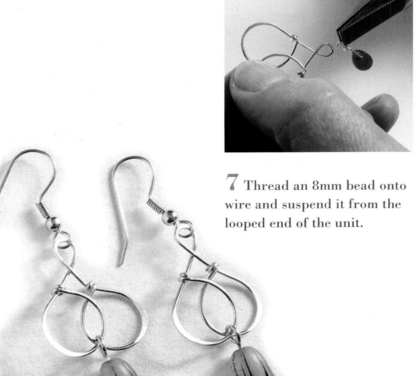

7 Thread an 8mm bead onto wire and suspend it from the looped end of the unit.

8 Connect a ready-made ear wire to the center top of the earring frame.

This variation is created in a similar way to the Art Deco design, but the ear wires have been attached to the central link instead.

Bead & Pearl Earrings

These simple, yet decorative, earrings with tiny seed pearls and transparent beads are perfect for both day and night. Using the same technique, you can encircle a variety of different sized and shaped beads to create stunning earrings, as well as necklace centerpieces; however, framing with small pearls does add an air of classic sophistication.

You will need

20-gauge (0.8 mm) and 28-gauge (0.4 mm) silver wire
Approx. 50 x size 9/0 pearl seed beads
2 x 8 mm light pink faceted beads
2 x 6 mm light pink faceted beads
2 x ready-made ear wires
Wire cutters
Round- and flat-nose pliers

1 For each earring, thread your 8 mm focal bead onto a spool of 20-gauge (0.8 mm) silver wire. Using your round-nose pliers, form a small link about ½ in. (1 cm) from the end of the wire (see page 11).

2 Curl the very tip of the wire around in the opposite direction to form a figure eight.

3 Cut the wire off the spool, leaving about ½ in. (1 cm) projecting beyond the bead. Form this projecting end into a link (see page 11).

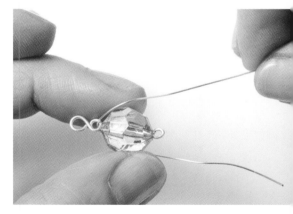

4 Thread 28-gauge (0.4 mm) silver wire through the bottom link of the figure eight, and bring the wire around the circumference of the bead to encircle it, leaving about 1½ in. (4 cm) of wire projecting at each end of the bead.

Create a matching necklace by following the earrings project and suspending from a beaded-spiral bail, hung on organza ribbon.

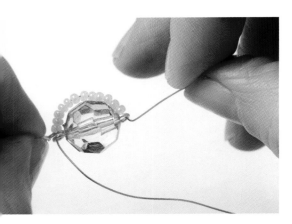 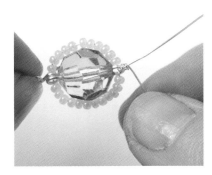 

5 Thread one side of the wire encircling the bead with pearl seed beads, then feed the wire through the bottom link of the focal bead. Feed more seed pearl beads onto the other end of the wire, until the bead is fully framed.

6 Thread each end of the beaded wire through opposite sides of the top link where they meet and twist together to secure. Cut one of the wires off, leaving only one remaining wire projecting.

7 Thread one more pearl seed bead onto the projecting stem, then create a wrapped loop and neaten all ends (see page 11).

8 Thread a 6mm light pink faceted bead onto 20-gauge (0.8mm) silver wire, creating a head pin at one end and a link at the other (see pages 11 and 12). Attach to the base link of the encircled beads. Finally, attach earring wires to the tops for suspension.

This gold-wire variation with a matching necklace omits the pendant drop bead. For the necklace, connect a loop of gold chain to each side of the centerpiece to frame the beads on either side.

Waterfall Chain Earrings

This is a great recycling project—a design that enables you to use up tiny lengths of broken silver chain, shimmering like sunlight shining on a waterfall. For a classic style, cut the chain into regular lengths or shape it to a tapered point. For a more contemporary fashion statement, make asymmetric units with different types of chain suspended at different levels.

You will need

24- and 20-gauge (0.6mm and 0.8mm) silver wire

Approx. 20 in. (50 cm) ready-made silver trace chain

28 red 8/0 seed beads

2 x ready-made ear wires

Wire cutters

Round- and flat-nose pliers

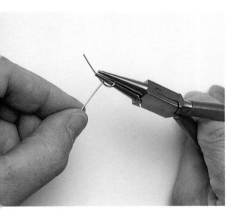

1 Cut a 2-in. (5-cm) length of 20-gauge (0.8mm) silver wire. Place your round-nose pliers in the center of the wire and twist the ends around in opposite directions, so that they cross over each other to form a loop.

2 Using your round-nose pliers, curl each end outward to form a small circle. You have now created the "hanger" for the waterfall chain.

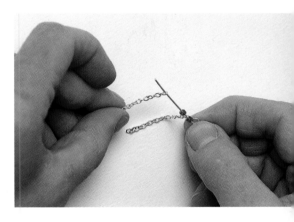

3 Cut a 1½-in. (4-cm) length of 20-gauge (0.8mm) wire and, using your round-nose pliers, make a link at one end (see page 11). Feed a red seed bead onto this wire and push it toward the link. Thread a small piece of ready-made chain onto the wire and push it toward the seed bead. Continue in this way, alternating chain and beads. The beads will keep the lengths of chain slightly separate from one another.

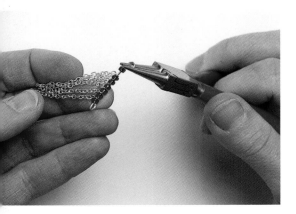

4 When you have used up eight seed beads and seven lengths of chain, curl the end of the wire into a link (see page 11).

5 Decide whether you want the chains to be the same length or to taper toward the center, and then cut to the desired length.

6 Using 24-gauge (0.6mm) wire, make seven jump rings (see page 14). Thread each jump ring with a single red seed bead.

7 Connect one beaded jump ring to the end of each of the suspended chains and press closed with flat-nose pliers.

8 Make two more jump rings out of 20-gauge (0.8mm) wire and connect the hanger unit made in Steps 1 and 2 to the suspended-chain unit.

9 Thread a seed bead onto a 1-in. (2.5-cm) piece of wire and make a link at one end and a head pin at the other (see pages 11 and 12). Using your flat-nose pliers, connect the linked bead to the center of the hanger unit. Repeat Steps 1–9 for the second earring, then attach the earring units to ready-made ear wires.

The chains on these earrings are shaped rather than all the same length. The matching necklace is made by making one of the earring units and attaching to a chain with a jump ring. Here, the chain is interspersed with threaded beads.

Chapter 3

Classic Chic

Elegant yet simple designer earrings can be a great conversation opener at any social gathering or society event. Once you've made the earrings in this chapter, you will be able to create matching necklaces, too!

Stick-Twist Earrings

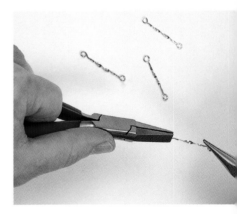

These elegantly classic earrings are not difficult to make. You may prefer to make them in one color of wire only. To make a matching necklace, simply create a number of the stick-twist units—about fourteen—and link them using jump rings to make a chain. Finish with a fish-hook clasp.

You will need

20-gauge (0.8mm) silver-plated wire
20-gauge (0.8mm) gold-plated wire
2 x 4mm gold-plated beads
4 x 4mm silver-plated beads
2 x ready-made ear wires
Wire cutters
Round-, chain-, and flat-nose pliers
Hammer and steel stake

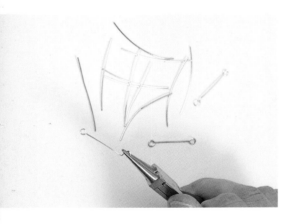

1 Cut six 1½-in. (4-cm) lengths of 20-gauge (0.8mm) wire—two of gold and four of silver-plated. Use your flat-nose pliers to straighten each length, then form a link at each end of each wire (see page 11).

2 Gently hammer the stem of each unit on a steel block, avoiding the links at the ends. This will flatten and spread the wire in the center of the unit—but make sure you don't hit your fingers!

3 Using flat-nose and chain-nose pliers, firmly grip the links at each end. Twist both pliers around two or three times, making sure that the links finish facing the same direction. (Do not over-twist—you may weaken the units just under the links and they will break off.)

4 Thread the 4mm gold and silver beads onto 20-gauge (0.8mm) wire, forming a link at each end (see page 11). Connect the gold beads to the silver twisted stalks and the silver ones to the gold twists. Make three large jump rings for each earring and connect them together in a chain. Attach one twist to each jump ring (two silver and one gold twist for each earring), then attach a ready-made ear wire to the top jump ring.

Bead Cage Earrings

These miniature wire cages can be filled with shells, rock chips, crystals, fabric scraps, ribbon, scented pot-pourri, dried rosebuds, and, of course, beads! The ½-in. (1-cm) diameter beads used in this project needed approximately 6 in. (15 cm) of 20-gauge (0.8mm) wire for each cage.

1 The length of the wire required for the cage is dependent on the size of the bead. Using the tips of your round-nose pliers, begin by forming a small circle at each end of the wire, curling it in opposite directions.

You will need

- 20-gauge (0.8mm) gold-plated wire
- 2 x 12mm round faceted beads
- 2 x ready-made gilt ear wires
- Wire cutters
- Round- and flat-nose pliers

2 Holding one of the small circles in the jaws of your flat-nose pliers, carefully curl the wire around itself to form a neat, flat spiral. Repeat at the other end, curling the wire in the opposite direction.

3 Continue coiling the wire into spirals at each end, ensuring they are a similar diameter, until they meet each other in the center (like an "S" shape).

4 When the all the wire has been used and both spirals are formed and touching each other, fold one spiral on top of the other and flatten, using flat-nose pliers.

5 Carefully pull the central circles out from each spiral at right angles, by placing the round-nose pliers on the central spiral.

6 Gently pull out these loops, extending the spiral and prizing open the spaces between each coil, using both pairs of pliers. Even out the spaces between the spirals.

7 Using your fingers, carefully prize open the center of the cage and place your selected bead in the middle of the extended wire spiral.

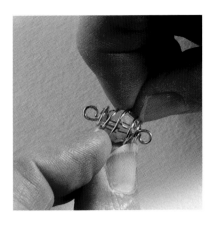  

8 Press the wire cage gently around the bead and even out the coils. Use your fingers for this stage, as pliers could bend the wire.

9 Using flat-nose pliers, fold one of the spiral ends in, next to the encased bead.

10 Make another identical caged bead. Suspend each from a ready-made earwire.

For added interest, why not create a second bead cage for each earring? It is also easy to make a matching necklace with linked bead cages.

Wiggly Wire Earrings

A gloriously delicate design for both day and evening wear. The colorful beads and fine wire units form a striking, yet understated design that suits all ages.

You will need

20-gauge (0.8mm) silver wire

2 beads of your choice

Wire cutters

Round-, chain-, and flat-nose pliers

Hammer and steel stake

1 Working from a spool of 20-gauge (0.8mm) silver wire, make a link at the end of the wire (see page 11) using your round-nose pliers.

2 Place the tips of your round-nose pliers just under this link and bend the wire around one shaft of the pliers.

3 Move your pliers about ½ in. (1 cm) up the wire and bend the wire around the shaft again, to create a wiggly shape in the wire.

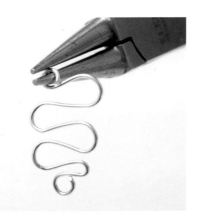

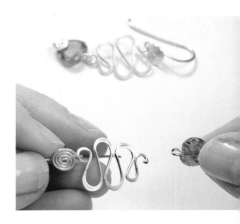

4 Repeat until you have created four more bends. Cut the wire from the spool and, using your round-nose pliers, form a link at the end (see page 11).

5 Push all the "wiggles" together so that they touch one another, then gently hammer the unit on a steel stake to work harden it (see page 13).

6 Create a spiral fish-hook ear wire (see page 15) and attach each wiggly earring unit to a drop bead. These small heart-shaped beads have been threaded with 20-gauge (0.8mm) silver wire. I created a spiral head pin at one end (see page 12) which I then folded over and flattened onto the top surface of the bead.

You could also create a long, continuous necklace, without a clasp, in this style. Alternatively, make a matching bracelet, suspending beads in between the "wiggly" units.

Wrapped Bead Earrings

This stylish design is perfect for using up inexpensive beads and turning them into something fantastic. Here blue beads are used with silver wire—a classic combination that always works well.

You will need

20-gauge (0.8mm) wire

2 x 12mm blue round faceted beads

2 x 4mm blue round faceted beads

2 x ready-made ear wires

Wire cutters

Round- and flat-nose pliers

1 For each earring, thread a 12mm bead onto a spool of 20-gauge (0.8mm) wire.

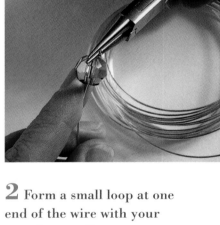

2 Form a small loop at one end of the wire with your round-nose pliers.

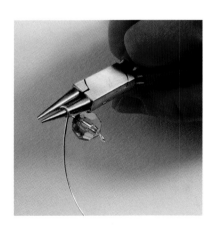

3 Twist the wire to form another loop at the other end of the bead and cut the wire off the spool, leaving about 6 in. (15 cm) of wire extending.

4 Wrap this wire around the bead in any fashion and as tightly as possible, using your fingers. Wrap it around the top and bottom of the bead as well.

5 Secure the end of the wire by wrapping it around one of the top loops, using your flat-nose pliers.

6 Using the very tips of your flat-nose pliers, carefully twist or tweak the wires to tighten them around the encased bead.

7 Thread the 4mm faceted beads with wire, creating a head pin at one end and a link at the other (see pages 11 and 12). Attach them to the base link of each earring after connecting the other ends to ear wires.

Fishy Fun Earrings

These easy-to-make earrings incorporate a simple fish shape filled in with beads in pink, salmon-like colors. The Celts commonly used stylized animal patterns, known as zoomorphs, in their designs, believing that they would thus miraculously be endowed with the animal's characteristics, and the salmon was associated with knowledge.

You will need

20-gauge (0.8mm) and 28-gauge (0.4mm) copper wire

Size 11/0 seed beads in pink/salmon colors

2 x 4mm copper-colored beads

2 x ready-made flat-backed earring posts and butterfly backs

Wire cutters

Round- and flat-nose pliers

Hammer and steel stake

Superglue

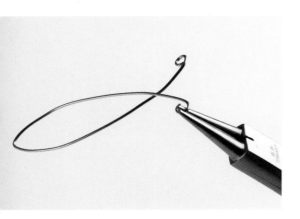

1 To make a salmon fish frame about 1¾ in. (4.5 cm) long, cut about 5 in. (13 cm) of 20-gauge (0.8mm) copper wire. Using the tips of your round-nose pliers, find the center of the wire and bend each side up until the wires cross over, about 2 in. (5 cm) from the end. Using the tips of your round-nose pliers, curl a small loop at the end of each wire.

2 Holding the loop firmly in your flat-nose pliers, form an open spiral (see page 13) on each side, curling outward, away from each other. Gently hammer the end of the spirals on a steel stake, avoiding the crossed-over wires.

3 Cut approximately 10 in. (25 cm) of 28-gauge (0.4mm) copper wire and wrap it several times around the crossed-over wires at the base of the spirals. Begin threading this fine wire with small seed beads, wrapping the wire around the top and bottom of the frame to fill the void.

4 Thread a 4 mm copper bead onto the wire to make the "eye" and secure the end of the wire around the frame. Cut off any excess wire and neaten the end (see page 11). Make a small closed spiral (see page 11) with a link and superglue an ear post to the back. Loop the link on the spiral over the "head" of the fish. Repeat all steps to make the second earring.

A matching fish pendant can complete the set. Suspend from a cord or chain for a fun birthday present for any friend with a Pisces birthsign!

Charm Cascade Earrings

Cascading down like bubbles in a waterfall, the beads are encased in spirals of wire to form a unified bunch. I used relatively small beads, to keep the design light and delicate. To encase larger beads, simply increase the amount of wire that you use.

You will need

20-gauge (0.8mm) silver-plated wire

6 x 6mm round hematite (or black glass) beads

2 x 4mm silver round beads

2 x ready-made ear wires

Wire cutters

Round- and flat-nose pliers

1 Cut about 6 in. (15 cm) of 20-gauge (0.8mm) silver wire. Find the center of the wire, and twist it around the tips of your round-nose pliers to form a little circle.

2 Holding the wire tightly in your flat-nose pliers, curl one end to create an open spiral approximately the same size as the beads that you are going to encase. Spiral the other end of the wire in the same way, making sure that each side curls in the opposite direction, like the letter "S."

3 Place a 6mm round hematite bead firmly against one of the spirals, and fold the opposite spiral over it to encase it.

4 Using your flat-nose pliers, pull the central loop of the spiral upright to make a suspension link, and spend a little time making sure that the wire sits tightly and evenly around the bead. Use your fingers to mold the wire around each bead so that it is snugly encased.

5 Once you have encased all the hematite beads, make two spirals (see page 13) and thread each with a 4mm silver bead before forming a top link (see page 11). Make about 16 jump rings (see page 14). Link the jump rings together in two short chains of eight rings each.

6 For each earring, attach three caged beads and one spiral to a jump-ring chain, spacing them evenly to form a cascade. Attach the top jump ring of the chain to a ready-made ear wire, customized with a matching 4mm hematite bead.

This design could also be used to create a matching necklace with a caged bead centerpiece. Alternatively, the beaded cascades can be made into dangling key-rings.

Chapter 4

Historic Charm

Create earrings that are inspired by past cultures and civilizations, the designs of which are timeless and will never date.

Greek Key Earrings

If you've never made a square unit like this classic Greek key symbol before, practice on a length of spare wire before using your good silver wire. It usually takes a couple of attempts to create even geometric pieces, but once you've mastered the technique, this is an easy jewelry design to make.

You will need

20-gauge (0.8mm) silver-plated
  wire
2 x 4mm round silver beads
2 x ready-made silver ear wires
Wire cutters
Round- and flat-nose pliers
Hammer and steel stake

1 Depending on the size of each geometric unit, cut about seven 4½–5-in (11.5–12.5-cm) lengths of 20-gauge (0.8mm) wire.

2 With the tips of your round-nose pliers, curl the ends of these wires into tiny hooks and squeeze these flat on themselves, as you would to make a head pin (see page 12).

3 Using narrow flat-nose pliers, bend the wire around at right angles, each time ensuring that the bend is folded just past the last, thereby creating an even space around the square.

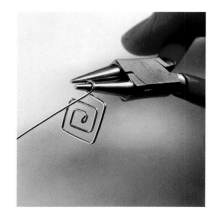

4 At about the tenth bend, when you have approximately 1½ in. (4 cm) of unbent wire remaining, form a small link by curling the wire around your round-nose pliers, crossing it over, and bringing it down to form the outer side of the square.

5 Create another link at the end of the wire in the same way, opposite the link on the other side of the square.

6 Flatten and gently tap each unit with your hammer (be careful not to hammer the cross-over link or you will weaken the wire).

7 Create a smaller geometric wire square, following Steps 1 to 4. Thread a 4mm silver bead onto the projecting wire, and secure with a link.

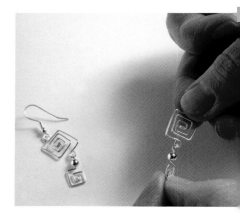

8 Connect this beaded unit to the large geometric square and suspend from an ear wire. Repeat for the second earring.

The Ancient Greeks and Turks used beads painted with the symbol of an eye (above left and opposite) to ward off evil spirits and to protect themselves from harm. For an authentic touch, include "eye" beads in your jewelry.

Book of Kells Earrings

I took my inspiration for these earrings from the *Book of Kells,* an illuminated manuscript now housed in the library of Trinity College, Dublin, that dates back more than 1200 years and is regarded as one of the greatest surviving treasures of Celtic art. The "stone" represents the stones from which the monks would have ground their colors. The pink wire unit represents the swirling framework and lavish ornamentation of the illuminated text.

You will need
20-gauge (0.8mm) pink wire
20-gauge (0.8mm) silver-plated wire
2 x 5mm pearl beads
2 x ready-made ear wires
Wire cutters
Round- and flat-nose pliers
Jig with 5 small, 1 medium, and
   1 large peg
Hammer and steel stake

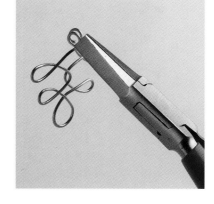

1 Cut two 7-in. (18-cm) lengths of 20-gauge (0.8mm) pink wire. Following the pattern on page 126, place the pegs in your jig. Using your round-nose pliers, form a loop at one end of the first length of wire and pull it tightly around the first peg. Now loop the wire around the remaining pegs, following the pattern. Snip off any excess wire.

A choker necklace can be created by wiring the two jig units together and attaching a centerpiece of your choice.

2 Gently flatten the wire unit on a steel stake with a hammer, being very careful not to remove the color coating on the wire. Repeat Steps 1 and 2 to make a second unit.

4 Create two silver jump rings (see page 14) and thread with the pearl beads. Attach one to the central space at the base of each unit, so that it is framed within the base loop. Attach a ready-made ear wire to the top of each unit.

3 Using your flat-nose pliers, twist the top two links through 90°, so that they face each other.

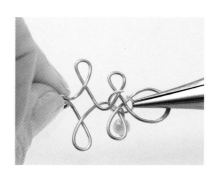

Egyptian Earrings

The technique used in this Egyptian-style project is a quick, yet very effective, way of creating wire jewelry with the appearance of chain mail. You could also experiment with making different combinations of looped rows, to design either rectangular or square pieces.

You will need
20-gauge (0.8mm) gold-plated
    wire
8 x 4mm gold-colored beads
2 x 10mm gold-colored beads
2 x ready-made gilt ear wires
Wire cutters
Round- and flat-nose pliers
Hammer and steel stake

1 For each earring, working from a coil of 20-gauge (0.8mm) wire, form a small loop at one end by curling it around the tips of your round-nose pliers.

2 Reposition your pliers beside the first loop and form another loop. The top wire should twist over the lower wire in the same direction as the first loop.

3 Continue shaping the wire into loops around the jaws of the pliers, until you have formed a row of seven complete circular loops.

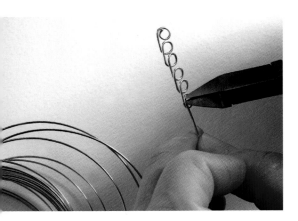  

4 Using wire cutters, snip off the loops from the coil, giving you a row of loops.

5 Repeat Steps 1 to 4 to create another wire row with six circles, then make rows with five, four, three, and finally two circles.

6 Very gently flatten the pieces, by tapping them with a hammer. Be careful not to hammer where the wires cross as this will weaken the wire.

7 Make approximately 16 jump rings (see page 14). Connect all looped rows together at their ends in descending order, using 9 jump rings for each unit.

8 Thread all the gold colored beads with 20-gauge (0.8mm) gold-colored wire, forming a head pin at one end and a link at the other (see pages 11 and 12) and connect to the base row of loops, with the 10mm bead in the center. Finally, attach the top jump ring of each earring to a ready-made ear wire.

Edwardian Earrings

This design of these elegant Edwardian-style earrings takes its inspiration from the early twentieth century. You could replace the pearls with crystal beads and the gold wire with silver to suit the fabrics or colors of your outfit. They are also perfect for wedding, prom, or formal evening wear.

You will need

20-gauge (0.8mm) gold-plated wire
2 x 6mm round pearls
2 x 6mm oval pearl beads
2 x size 9/0 clear glass seed beads
2 x ready-made gilt ear wires
Wire cutters
Round- and flat-nose pliers

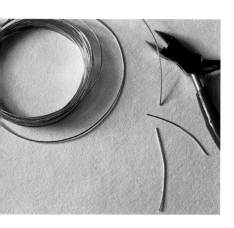

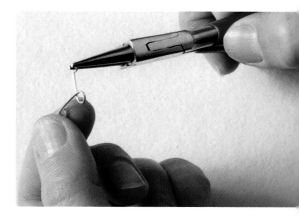

1 The central beaded pendant is constructed first. To make this, cut two 2-in. (5-cm) lengths of 20-gauge (0.8mm) gold-plated wire.

2 Using round-nose pliers, find the center of each wire and cross one side over the other to create a central loop.

3 Curl the extended ends outward into small loops using the ends of the round-nose pliers. These will make up the two halves of the "hanger."

4 Create jump rings to link the pendant together by wrapping 20-gauge (0.8mm) wire around the round-nose pliers to form a spring (see page 14). Cut each ring of the spring to create the links.

5 Connect the two halves of the hanger together on each side, using the jump rings you have just made.

6 Thread the round and oval pearls with 20-gauge (0.8mm) wire, creating a link at each end (see page 11). Make a closed spiral (see page 13), topped with a clear seed bead to suspend at the base of the earrings.

7 Attach a ready-made ear wire to the top of each hanger. Attach the round pearl between the hangers and then add the oval pearl and the spiral to the base to complete the dangle droplet.

Create an elegant matching pendant following all the steps of the earrings project.

Triskele Earrings

The triskele, or triskelion, is a motif consisting of three interlocking spirals. The number three was very important to the Celts, as it stood for the on-going cycle of birth, life, and death—so this design has strong symbolic links to Celtic culture and history.

You will need

20-gauge (0.8mm) pink wire
20-gauge (0.8mm) purple wire
2 x ready-made flat-backed
   earring posts and butterfly
   backs
Wire cutters
Round- and flat-nose pliers
Superglue

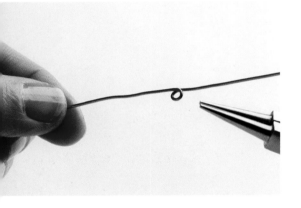

1 Cut a 6-in (5-cm) length of 20-gauge (0.8mm) pink wire. Find the center of the wire and carefully twist it around the tips of your round-nose pliers to form a little circle.

2 Using your flat-nose pliers, curl each end of the wire into an open spiral (see page 13), curling in opposite directions like the letter "S."

3 Cut a 5-in (12.5-cm) length of 20-gauge (0.8mm) pink wire and form another spiral the same diameter as the first two, leaving a tail of wire about 2 in. (5 cm) long.

4 Thread this tail of wire through the central loop of the double spiral and wrap it two or three times around the central loop to secure. You should be left with about 1½ in. (4 cm) of wire protruding.

5 Using your round-nose pliers, form a small loop at the end of this protruding wire. Hold the loop in your flat-nose pliers and curl the wire into a closed spiral (see page 13). Press the spiral flat against the center of the triskele motif to hide the wrapped wires underneath. If necessary, adjust the shape of the spirals using your fingers and flat-nose pliers.

6 Create a closed spiral (see page 13) and glue a ready-made flat-backed earring post to the back, so that you can suspend the triskele motif. Repeat all steps to make the second earring.

Hieroglyphic Earrings

The wire "hieroglyphs" on these earrings are ones that I devised myself, but you can use any wiggly wire pattern of your own creation. Experiment and develop your own wire shapes, so that your earrings are completely unique!

You will need

20-gauge (0.8mm) silver-plated wire

2 x 4mm red beads

2 x ready-made ear wires

Wire cutters

Round- and flat-nose pliers

1 Working from a spool of 20-gauge (0.8mm) wire, make a little hook at the end of the wire using your round-nose pliers. Coil this wire around itself in a spiral, holding it steady with your flat-nose pliers.

2 Bend the wire around the tip of your round-nose pliers to create a wiggly shape.

3 Bend the wire around the outline of the wiggly shape as a frame. Cut the wire off the spool, leaving enough to thread on a bead plus about ½ in. (1 cm). Bend the extending wire at 90°.

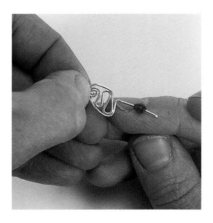

4 Feed a 4mm red bead onto the extending wire and push it up to the bend in the wire.

5 Using your round-nose pliers, make a link at the end of the extending wire (see page 11).

The hieroglyph units can easily be attached to ready-made chain to make a unique necklace. For a more casual and informal-looking style, make the hieroglyphs in colored wire.

6 Attach the hieroglyph squiggles to ready-made ear wires.

Chapter 5

Glitz & Glamour

We all need a little bit of "bling" to cheer up a party outfit, or to add some sparkle to our lives! Have fun using faceted crystals and bright colored beads in any of the earring designs.

Starburst Earrings

Inspired by Indian "Bollywood" style, these hoop earrings look exotic and flamboyant, with the "dangles" radiating out from the central star bead like trails of light. The circular pendant can be increased in size to make a matching necklace.

You will need

20-gauge (0.8mm) silver wire

20 x 4mm and 2 x 6mm round silver beads

2 x ½-in. (1-cm) silver star beads

2 x 8mm, 4 x 6mm, and 2 x 4mm purple faceted plastic crystal beads

Assorted purple seed beads

2 x ready-made ear wires

Wire cutters

Round- and flat-nose pliers

Circular mandrel, 1 in. (2.5 cm) in diameter

1 Working from a spool of 20-gauge (0.8mm) wire, wrap the wire twice around the mandrel to form two complete circles. (I used a section of wooden curtain pole as my "mandrel," but any cylindrical object the right size will do.)

2 Cut through the coils in the same way as when making jump rings (see page 14), to make two large circles.

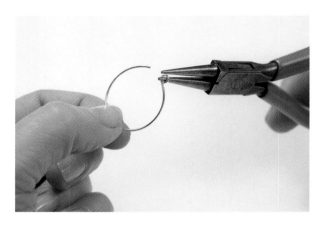

3 Cut five lengths of 20-gauge (0.8mm) wire for each earring. I cut two ½-in. (1-cm) lengths for the outer rays, two 2-in. (5-cm) lengths for the inner rays, and one central stem about 3 in. (7.5 cm) long—the length depends on the size of your beads. Following the photograph, thread on your beads, then form one end of the wire into a head pin and the other into a link (see pages 11 and 12).

4 Using round-nose pliers, form a link (see page 12) at one end of each large wire circle.

5 Following the photograph, thread your beads and beaded "rays" onto the circular frames, suspending the long beaded ray in the center of each earring.

6 Using round-nose pliers, form a second link (see page 11) at the other end of the frame. Push the two ends of the frame together, then twist the top links through 90° with your flat-nose pliers, so that they face each other.

7 Make two small jump rings (see page 14) from 20-gauge (0.8mm) wire. Open them up. Hook each one through the link at the top of a star bead, then close the links tightly with your flat-nose pliers.

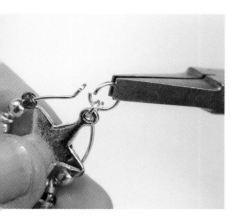

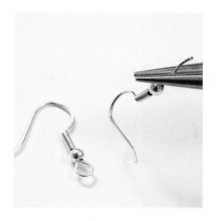

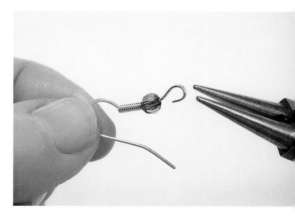

8 Make two large jump rings (see page 14) from 20-gauge (0.8mm) wire. Open them up. Hook one through the first link on one circular frame, then through the star bead jump ring, and finally through the second link on the frame. Close the jump ring. Repeat to complete the second earring.

9 Undo the link at the end of the ready-made ear wires, straighten out the wire, and remove any beads.

10 Slide a 4mm faceted purple crystal bead onto each ear wire, and then re-make the link.

11 Undo the large jump ring at the top of the starburst piece, hook it through the jump ring at the base of the ear wire, and then close the link again with your flat-nose pliers.

You can suspend any bead or charm at the center of these earrings and create a much simpler design using fewer pendant rays.

Far Eastern Earrings

With their simple curves, reminiscent of temple roofs and Chinese and Japanese calligraphy, these earrings have a distinct flavor of the Orient. The hammering technique does take practice—but, as they say, practice makes perfect! If you find you've made a real mess of it, shape the ends of the hammered wires into little curls; the result will not look so Oriental, but it still will be very striking!

You will need

18-gauge (1mm) silver-plated wire
2 x ready-made ear wires
Wire cutters
Round- and flat-nose pliers
Dowels 1¼ in. (3 cm) and ¾ in. (2 cm)
  in diameter
Hammer and steel stake

1 Cut four 1½-in. (4-cm) and two 1-in (2.5-cm) lengths of wire. Shape the large pieces around the larger dowel and the small pieces around the smaller dowel.

2 Gently hammer one end of each curved wire on a steel stake until it spreads to a bulbous, paddle-shaped tip. Hammer both sides.

3 Using your round-nose pliers, curl all the unhammered ends into links (see page 11). Make sure that the longer curves have links that curl in the opposite direction to the two shorter curves.

4 Make two large jump rings (see page 14). Attach two long and one short curved unit to each jump ring, making sure that the longer units curve in toward the shorter length, so that they will cross over each other when suspended. Suspend each unit from a ready-made ear wire.

Belly Dancer Earrings

Dangling silver and gold coin decorations give these earrings an exotic flavor! Why not make a matching bracelet, by connecting looped units into a chain, using jump rings? You could also extend the bracelet into a necklace by attaching a piece of ready-made chain to each side.

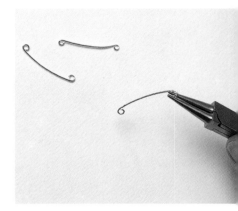

You will need

20-gauge wire (0.8mm) silver-plated wire

2 gold- and 2 silver-colored metal "coin-like" decorations about ½ in. (1.5 cm) in diameter

2 x ready-made ear wires

Wire cutters

Round- and flat-nose pliers

1 Cut four 1½-in (4-cm) and two 3½-in (9-cm) lengths of 20-gauge (0.8mm) silver wire. Using the tips of your round-nose pliers, make a small loop at each end, curling them in toward each other.

2 Find the center of each short looped wire and mold it around the widest part of your round-nose pliers, making sure the loops curl outward on each side. On the two longer wires, place your pliers one third of the way in from each end and form a double "wiggle" in the wire.

3 Make five jump rings for each earring (see page 14). Connect the coins together in pairs, with one gold and one silver coin in each pair.

4 Using jump rings, connect all the units together as shown and suspend from a ready-made ear wire.

These looped units can be connected in many different configurations, chains for necklaces and bracelets and suspended with matching "coins" or beads of your choice.

Cupid Earrings

The pinkish tone of the copper is intended to evoke Cupid, the chubby, pink cherub of love who strikes us with his loaded arrows just when we're least expecting it! These earring units can be turned into a continuous chain-link design that would work well as a bracelet or necklace.

You will need

20-gauge (0.8 mm) copper wire
2 x 4mm lilac bicone crystals
2 x 6mm purple bicone crystals
2 x ready-made copper fish-hook
   ear wires
Wire cutters
Round- and flat-nose pliers
Hammer and steel stake

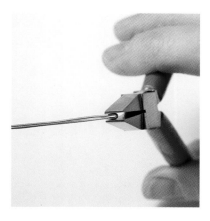

1 For each earring, cut one piece of 20-gauge (0.8mm) copper wire, about 4–4½ in. (10–12 cm) long. Fold each wire in half. Squeeze the end of the doubled wires together with your flat-nose pliers and straighten out the wires with your fingers so that they run parallel to one another.

2 Using the tips of your round-nose pliers, form a small loop at the doubled-over end of the wire, curling the wire toward you so that the loop sits at right angles to the straight wires.

3 Holding the doubled loop firmly in the jaws of your flat-nose pliers, gently pull the two wires apart.

4 Place the widest part of your round-nose pliers on each side of the doubled loop and bring the wires back down until they meet and cross over, forming a heart-shaped frame.

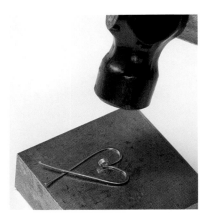

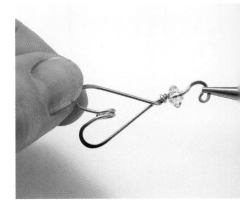

5 Gently "stroke" hammer (see page 13) the round shoulders of the frame, taking care not to hammer and squash the doubled loop.

6 Wrap one of the extending wires at the base two or three times around the other. Snip off any excess wrapped wire and squeeze the end flat against the stem with your flat-nose pliers to neaten, leaving the other wire extending.

7 Thread the projecting wire with the 4mm lilac crystal and make a small spiral head pin at the end (see page 12).

This heart unit can be created as a chain for necklace and bracelet designs.

8 Thread the 6mm purple crystal onto 20-gauge (0.8mm) wire and form a head pin at one end and a link at the other (see pages 11 and 12). Attach the crystal to the doubled wire loop from Step 2. Make three jump rings (see page 14) and join them into a chain. Attach the top jump ring to an ear wire and the bottom one to the doubled wire loop.

Tassel Earrings

Chained tassels are simple to make and as well as making dangly earrings, they're perfect for necklace centerpieces and bracelet charms. You can also adapt them for home furnishings and sew them onto the corners of cushion covers or the ends of curtain tiebacks. Or why not use a tassel as a fabulous key ring or purse charm?

You will need

50-in. (120-cm) length of ready-made chain

20-gauge (0.8mm) and 28-gauge (0.4mm) silver wire

2 x 8mm turquoise barrel tube beads

2 x 4mm round silver beads

1 x 1cm bicone silver bead

10 x size 9/0 turquoise seed beads

10 x size 9/0 black seed beads

2 x ready-made ear wires

Wire cutters

Round- and flat-nose pliers

1 For each earring, cut ten 2½-in (6-cm) lengths of ready-made chain.

2 Thread the top link of each length of chain onto a 3-in. (7.5-cm) length of 28-gauge (0.4mm) silver wire.

3 Bring the two ends of the wire together and twist them together to form a short stem about ¼ in. (0.5 cm) long, above the rows of chain.

4 Thread the 8mm turquoise bead and then the 4mm silver bead onto the twisted stem. Using your round- and flat-nose pliers, make a wrapped loop, with the doubled wire at the top of the bead hole.

5 Thread the 1 cm silver bead onto 20-gauge (0.8mm) silver wire. Using your round-nose pliers, make a link at each end (see page 11).

6 Connect the tassel to one link of the 1cm bicone silver colored bead.

7 Thread five black and five turquoise size 9/0 seed beads individually onto 20-gauge (0.8mm) silver wire. Form a link at one end and a head pin at the other (see pages 11 and 12).

8 Alternating black and turquoise seed beads, attach one seed bead to each section of the chain tassel by opening the link on the seed bead, looping it through the bottom link of one section of chain, and closing the link again with your flat-nose pliers. Attach to ready-made ear wires.

You can create your own spiral fish-hook ear wires (see page 15) to customize your design. The chained tassel design can also look extremely distinctive as the centerpiece of a corded necklace.

Orbital Earrings

These wire wreaths have a plain silver bead in the center to add interest, but you could equally leave out the central bead; "hoop" earrings are always popular. Having grasped the technique of making the wreath, you could make a larger version as a decorative napkin ring.

You will need
20-gauge (0.8mm) silver wire
2 x 8mm silver-colored teardrop beads
2 x ready-made ear wires
Wire cutters
Round- and flat-nose pliers
Cylindrical mandrel approx. ¾ in. (2 cm) in diameter
Hammer and steel stake

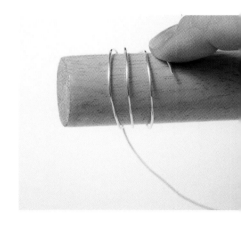

1 For each earring, working from a spool of 20-gauge (0.8mm) silver wire, wrap the wire three times around a cylindrical mandrel about ¾ in. (2 cm) in diameter. Cut the wire from the spool, leaving about 12 in. (30 cm) projecting.

2 Wrap the shorter cut end of the wire around the loops of wire to secure them as one neat circle. Neaten the ends (see page 11).

3 Wrap the long projecting wire around the circular frame, leaving one wrap very loose to provide a gap from which you can suspend the ear wires.

4 When all the wire has been used up, neaten the ends (see page 11). Place the unit on a steel stake and hammer both sides to flatten and work harden the wire.

A matching pendant can be
made using the same
technique with an added tassel
(see Tassel Earrings on page
103, steps 1–4).

5 Loop a large jump ring (see
page 14) through a silver
teardrop bead and attach it to
the center of the circular unit.
Attach a ready-made ear wire
to the same jump ring.

Chapter 6

Celebrations & Occasions

Themed designs for Christmas, birthdays, and special days, such as Valentine's Day, are always required and can make great gifts for close friends and family. Some of these designs also look fabulous attached to the front of greetings cards— making a "gift card" all in one!

Birthstone Earrings

Make a gorgeous pair of earrings as a birthday present, personalizing them to include the recipient's birthstone (see chart, page 126). The semi-precious turquoise chip stones used in these earrings are purported to promote spiritual attunement and well being.

You will need

Ready-made silver chain
20-gauge (0.8mm) silver wire
2 x 6mm round turquoise beads
Approx. 88 x turquoise chip stones
2 x ready-made ear wires
Wire cutters
Round- and flat-nose pliers

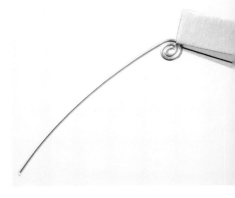

1 For each earring, cut two 5–6-in. (12.5–15-cm) lengths of ready-made chain. Make a jump ring from 20-gauge (0.8mm) silver wire (see page 14) and thread it through one end of each section of chain to join them together.

2 Thread two turquoise chips onto the end of a spool of 20-gauge (0.8mm) silver wire. Leave about ½ in. (1 cm) protruding on each side of the beads and cut the wire off the spool.

3 Take the chips off the wire. Form a small spiraled head pin at one end of the wire (see page 13). Straighten the other end of the wire if necessary.

4 Count three chain links down from the jump ring on one side of the chain and slide the pin into the link from the outside. Rethread the pin with the two turquoise chips and then slide it through the third link on the opposite side of the chain.

5 Form a spiraled head pin on the other end of the pin to hold the chips in place.

6 Repeat Steps 2–5 along the length of the earring, increasing the chips on each unit to three and then four, or five. Decrease the number of chips at the end of the earring. Leave three links of the chain between each beaded unit.

7 When the earring is full, join the two chains by attaching a jump ring to the chain ends. Position the jump ring three chain links from the last beaded unit, as shown.

8 Thread the 6mm round turquoise beads with wire, forming a head pin at one end and a link at the other (see pages 11 and 12). Attach them to the base jump ring of the earrings. The top end is now ready to suspend from ready-made ear wires. Alternatively, create your own (see page 15).

The bracelet and earrings shown here are made using bugle and seed beads, creating a "ladder" effect. A fish-hook clasp and eye complete the bracelet.

Sweetheart Earrings

February is the time when sweethearts celebrate St Valentine's Day, so why not create a pair of heart-shaped earrings to wear? This design can be made without beads, using a thicker gauge or colored wire. The heart motif would also look great on the front of a card or gift tag or attached to a key ring.

You will need

20-gauge (0.8mm) silver wire

Approx. 120 x size 9/0 pink seed beads

2 x ready-made ear wires

Wire cutters

Round- and flat-nose pliers

Mandrel or cylindrical dowel approx. ½ in. (1 cm) in diameter

1 For each earring, cut a 6-in. (15-cm) length of 20-gauge (0.8mm) silver wire. Holding the center with the ends of your round-nose pliers, curl the two ends of the wire around the shaft to form a loop.

2 Place a mandrel or cylindrical dowel about ½ in. (1 cm) in diameter just by the central loop and bring the extending wires down on each side to form a heart shape.

3 Thread each side of the heart-shaped frame with size 9/0 pink seed beads, using approximately 30 beads on each side. Using your fingers, wrap one wire two or three times around the other at the base of the heart.

4 Snip off any excess wrapped wire and squeeze the end flat against the stem with your flat-nose pliers to neaten (see page 11), leaving the other wire extending.

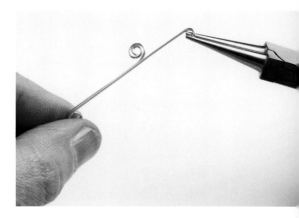

5 To form the top bail of the pendant, cut a 5-in. (12.5 cm) length of 20-gauge (0.8mm) silver wire and fold it in half, squeezing the ends together so that the doubled wires run parallel to each other.

6 Using the ends of your round-nose pliers, curl the doubled-up end of wire into a loop.

7 Holding the loop in your left hand, curl a spiral at each loose end of the wire, curling the spirals in opposite directions.

8 To complete the beaded heart frame, thread the projecting wire with two pink seed beads and spiral the end (see page 13).

9 Connect the doubled wire bail that you created in Steps 5–7 to two jump rings and attach to the center of the heart frame.

10 Fold the center of the doubled wire down over the heart shape and suspend from a ready-made ear wire. Repeat all steps to make the second earring.

To make a matching necklace, follow all the steps for the earrings and suspend the heart shape from satin ribbon.

Shooting Star Earrings

These earrings have a real Christmassy feel about then, although they can be worn all through the year, bringing a hint of Christmas magic to your everyday life! The "light trails" radiating out from the central star add extra sparkle and movement to the piece—but you could omit these and create a simple star shape.

You will need

20-gauge (0.8mm) silver wire
28-gauge (0.4mm) gold-plated wire
18 x 4mm round silver and gold beads

2 x ready-made ear wires
Wire cutters
Round- and flat-nose pliers
Hammer and steel stake

It would be easy to make this into a decorative lapel or hat pin by simply attaching the main earring unit to a lapel pin.

1 Working directly from a spool of 20-gauge (0.8mm) silver wire, use the tips of your round-nose pliers to form a link (see page 11) at the end of the wire. Place the tips of your pliers about ½ in. (1 cm) from this link and bend the wire back toward it, forming a V-shape.

2 Reposition the tips of your pliers level with the link you created in Step 1 and bend the wire back up in the opposite direction. Repeat to create six zig-zags. Cut the wire from the spool, leaving a small tail.

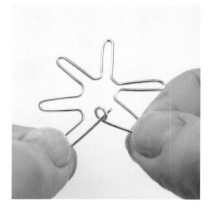

3 Using your fingers, pull each end around to form a circular shape. Using your flat-nose pliers, twist the end link so that it sits at 90° to the zig-zags. Thread the cut end of the wire into this link, and secure by looping the wire around the link. Neaten the ends. Adjust the zig-zags with your fingers to make a star.

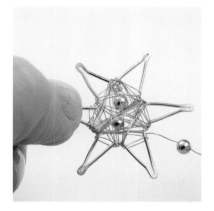

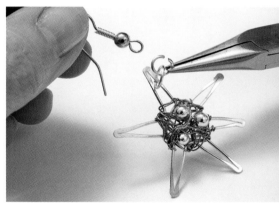

4 Using your flat-nose pliers, squeeze the ends of each zig-zag to form the points of your star. When you are satisfied with the overall shape, hammer the frame on a steel stake to work harden it (see page 13).

5 Cut about 12 in. (30 cm) of 28-gauge (0.4mm) gold-colored wire and wrap it around the center of the star frame in a freeform manner to form a fairly solid mass. Cut another length of wire and attach it in the same way, this time threading on small gold and silver beads as you wrap.

6 Once you are satisfied with the center of your star, attach one of the points to a couple of jump rings (see page 14) and suspend from a ready-made ear wire. Repeat all steps to make the second earring.

Holly-Leaf Earrings

This simple design can be increased or decreased in scale to suit your style. You can make the bicone crystal the main feature, or add silver beads as added detail. The holly motif can also be attached to satin ribbons and tied around napkins for an original festive table setting, or suspended on clear fishing line and hung in the window to catch the frosty sparkle of Yuletide!

You will need

20-gauge (0.8mm) and 28-gauge
  (0.4mm) silver wire
Approx. 28 x size 9/0 crystal
  seed beads
2 x 7mm bicone crystals
4 x 4mm silver beads (optional)
2 x 5mm silver beads
2 x ready-made ear wires
Wire cutters
Round- and flat-nose pliers
Hammer and steel stake

1 For each earring, working from a spool of 20-gauge (0.8 mm) wire, place the tips of your round-nose pliers 1 in. (2.5 cm) from the end and bend the wire at 90°.

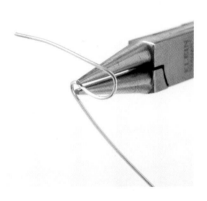

2 Place the widest part of your round-nose pliers just next to the bend in the wire and curve it around to form a U-shape.

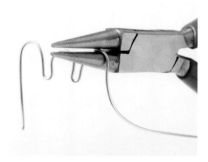

3 Repeat Steps 1 and 2 to make three more U-shapes, which will eventually form one side of the holly leaf.

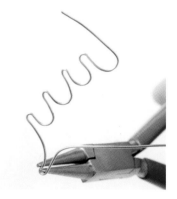

4 Make a fourth U-shape, slightly longer and more elongated than the previous ones; this will be the tip of the holly leaf.

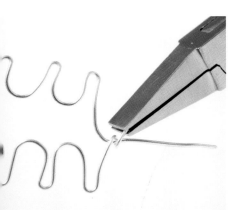

5 Bring the wire up and make four more U-shapes to form the opposite side of the leaf. Bring the wires together and wrap the cut end around the stem to secure. Cut the wire off the spool, leaving about 1 in. (2.5 cm) extending.

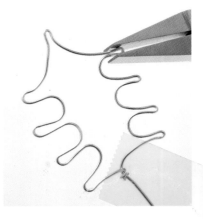

6 Using your flat-nose pliers, squeeze the tip of each U-shaped curve to create a slightly **more** spiky appearance, but **keep a** slightly open channel at **the** tip of the leaf. Adjust the overall shape with your fingertips if necessary.

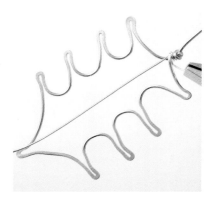

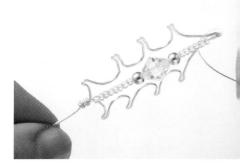

7 Gently hammer the outer frame of the leaf on a steel stake to work harden it, making sure you do not touch the wrapped wires of the stem.

8 Cut a piece of 28-gauge (0.4mm) silver wire about 1½ in. (4 cm) longer than the leaf. Wrap one end around the stem of the leaf to secure, and pull the wire down the center of the leaf frame.

9 Thread this fine wire with eight crystal seed beads, a 7mm bicone crystal, and then more crystal seed beads to fill the wire; you could add a 4mm silver bead before/after the bicone crystal (as above). Secure the wire at the end of the leaf in the channel (from Step 6). Snip off any excess. Neaten the ends (see page 11).

10 Thread a 5mm silver bead onto the stem and form a link at the other end of the bead hole using your round-nose pliers. Connect the jump ring at the base of a ready-made ear wire to this link.

Make a matching necklace, following all the earring steps, and suspend from a handmade chain.

Christmas Tree Earrings

These earrings are based on the triangular shape of a stylized Christmas tree. This is a quick and fun idea to make as a gift for friends and family. For the perfect pair of celebratory earrings, make it with colored green wire for the outer coil and a line of red, sparkling crystal beads down the center.

You will need

20-gauge (0.8mm) silver wire
0.5mm nylon filament
4 x 1mm silver crimp beads
6–8 freshwater rice pearls,
    5–8mm long
2 x ready-made silver ear wires
Wire cutters
Round-, flat-, and chain-nose
    pliers
Hammer and steel stake
    (optional)

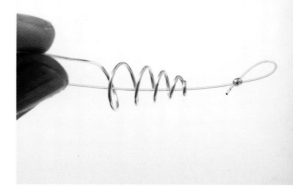

1 Using your round- and flat-nose pliers and working from a spool of 20-gauge (0.8mm) silver wire, form a closed spiral (see page 13) at least ½ in. (1 cm) in diameter. Cut the wire off the spool, leaving about 1 in. (2.5 cm) extending. If you wish, you can gently hammer the spiral on a steel stake to work harden it.

2 Push your round-nose pliers into the center of the spiral and pull the wire down with your fingers to form an evenly spaced, tapered coil.

3 Thread a length of nylon filament through the center of the coil, so that about 1 in. (2.5 cm) extends beyond each end. Thread a crimp bead onto the nylon filament above the narrow end of the coil and double the filament back through the crimp bead to form a loop. Squeeze the crimp bead tightly with your chain-nose pliers to secure it on the filament.

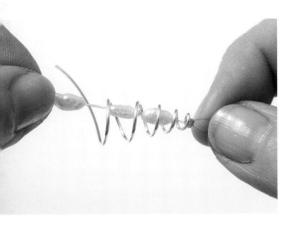

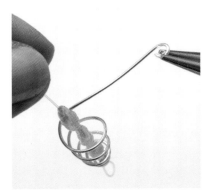

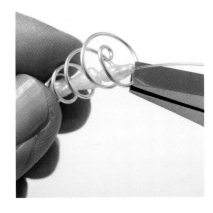

4 Thread the nylon filament inside the coil with freshwater pearls, right up to the last and widest coil.

5 Holding the filament firmly as you work, so that the beads cannot fall off, form a small circle at the end of the extending wire using the tips of your round-nose pliers.

6 Holding this circle firmly in your flat-nose pliers, spiral the wire around to form an open spiral that sits as a base to the tapered coil.

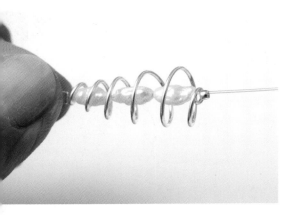

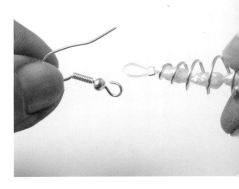

7 Thread the end of the nylon filament through the central circle of the base and feed on a crimp bead, pushing the crimp bead right up to the base of the spiral.

8 Squeeze the crimp bead tightly with your chain-nose pliers to secure. Snip off any excess filament.

9 Repeat Steps 1–8 to make a second "tree." Attach the loop at the top of each "tree" to a ready-made ear wire.

For a really festive-looking party piece, use Christmassy red and green beads.

Earrings Gallery

Here are some more examples of my earring designs, which I hope will inspire you to develop your own ideas.

Jig Pattern

This pattern is based on a jig in which the holes are arranged in horizontal rows. If your jig has holes arranged on the diagonal, simply rotate it until the holes are aligned as shown below. For more information on using a jig, turn to page 10.

Book of Kells Earrings (page 78)
Curl the wire around the pegs as shown, following the arrows and returning to the center peg between 2 and 3, and 5 and 6.

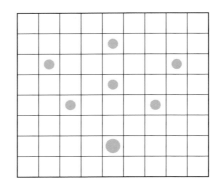

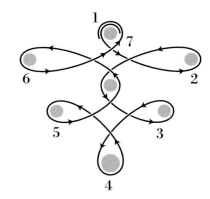

Birthstone Chart

This chart provides a guide to birthstones you can use, as shown in the Birthstone Earrings on page 110; you could also incorporate birthstones into other designs within this book.

Month and zodiac sign	Semi-precious stone	Color	Month and zodiac sign	Semi-precious stone	Color
JANUARY Jan. 1–19 (Capricorn) Jan. 20–31 (Aquarius)	Garnet	Deep red/burgundy	**JULY** July 1–22 (Cancer) July 23–31 (Leo)	Ruby	Bright red
FEBRUARY Feb. 1–18 (Aquarius) Feb. 19–28 (Pisces)	Amethyst	Purple	**AUGUST** August 1–22 (Leo) August 23–31 (Virgo)	Peridot	Pale green
MARCH March 1–20 (Pisces) March 21–31 (Aries)	Aquamarine	Pale blue	**SEPTEMBER** Sept. 1–22 (Virgo) Sept. 23–30 (Libra)	Sapphire	Pale blue
APRIL April 1–19 (Aries) April 20–30 (Taurus)	Diamond/clear crystal	Clear/colorless	**OCTOBER** Oct. 1–23 (Libra) Oct. 24–31 (Scorpio)	Opal	Variegated/multi-colored
MAY May 1–20 (Taurus) May 21–31 (Gemini)	Emerald	Green	**NOVEMBER** Nov. 1–21 (Scorpio) Nov. 22–30 (Sagittarius)	Topaz	Yellow
JUNE June 1–21 (Gemini) June 22–30 (Cancer)	Pearl	Cream	**DECEMBER** Dec. 1–21 (Sagittarius) Dec. 22–31 (Capricorn)	Turquoise	Bright blue

Useful Addresses

Wirejewellery.co.uk
Faulkners Oast (East)
Tonbridge Road
Hadlow, Kent TN11 0AJ
Tel: 01732 850 727
www.wirejewellery.co.uk
Author's website: workshops, DVDs, and expert advice.

The Wireworkers Guild
www.wireworkersguild.blogspot.com
Founded by Linda Jones, this is a free forum for exchanging and sharing ideas, techniques, and design inspiration.

US suppliers

Fire Mountain Gems
1 Fire Mountain Way
Grants Pass, OR 97526–2373
Tel: 800-355-2137
www.firemountaingems.com

Jewelry Supply
Roseville, CA 95678
Tel: 916-780-9610
www.jewelrysupply.com

Land of Odds
718 Thompson Lane
Ste 125, Nashville, TN 37204
Tel: 615-292-0610
www.landofodds.com

Michaels
www.michaels.com
Visit the website for store locations nationwide.

Mode International Inc
5111–4th Avenue
Brooklyn, NY 11220
Tel: 718-765-0124
www.modebeads.com

Rings & Things
PO Box 450
Spokane, WA 99210–0450
Tel: 800-366-2156
www.rings-things.com

Rio Grande
7500 Bluewater Road, NW
Albuquerque, NM 87121
Tel: 800-545-6566
www.riogrande.com

Shipwreck Beads
8650 Commerce Place Drive NE
Lacey, WA 98516
Tel: 800-950-4232
www.shipwreckbeads.com

Stormcloud Trading Co.
725 Snelling Avenue North
St. Paul, MN 55104
Tel: 651-645-0343
www.beadstorm.com

Thunderbird Supply Company
1907 W. Historic Route 66
Gallup, NM 87301
Tel: 800-545-7968
www.thunderbirdsupply.com

Unicorne Beads
404 Evelyn Place, Suite D
Placentia, CA 92870
Tel: 714-572-8558
www.unicornebeads.com

Wig Jig
24165 IH-10 West, Suite 217-725
San Antonio, TX 78257-1160
Tel: 800-579-9473
www.wigjig.com

UK suppliers

The Bead Shop
21a Tower Street
London WC2H 9NS
Tel: 0207 240 0931
www.beadworks.co.uk

Cookson Precious Metals
59–83 Vittoria Street
Birmingham B1 3NZ
Tel: 0845 100 1122
www.cooksongold.com
Suppliers of steel stakes, jewelry tools, and precious metal wires.

Creative Beadcraft Ltd
1 Marshall Street
London W1F 9BA
Tel: 0207 734 1982
www.creativebeadcraft.co.uk

E-Beads Ltd
Unit TR1-2 Trowbray House
108 Weston Street
London SE1 3QB
Tel: 0207 367 6217
www.e-beads.co.uk

International Craft
Unit 4 The Empire Centre
Imperial Way, Watford
Hertfordshire WD24 4YH
Tel: 01923 235 336
www.internationalcraft.com

Jilly Beads Ltd
1 Anstable Road
Morecambe, Lancashire LA4 6TG
Tel: 01524 412 728
www.jillybeads.co.uk

Madcow Beads
The Bull Pen
Great Larkhill Farm
Long Newnton, Tetbury
Gloucestershire GL8 8SY
Tel: 0844 357 0943
www.madcowbeads.com
Suppliers of Tronex Cutters.

Wires.co.uk
18 Raven Road
London E18 1HW
Tel: 0208 505 0002
www.wires.co.uk
Suppliers of wire only.

Index

Acknowledgments

A warm and heartfelt thanks to Cindy Richards at CICO, for giving me another opportunity to have my designs in print. Also, a special thank you to Carmel Edmonds, who was instrumental in bringing the jumble of projects, text, and images together in a digestible new book!